Really *WILD*

CHIMPANZEES

Claire Robinson

Heinemann
LIBRARY

First published in Great Britain by Heinemann Library
Halley Court, Jordan Hill, Oxford, OX2 8EJ,
a division of Reed Educational and Professional Publishing Ltd

OXFORD FLORENCE PRAGUE MADRID ATHENS
MELBOURNE AUCKLAND KUALA LUMPUR SINGAPORE TOKYO
IBADAN NAIROBI KAMPALA JOHANNESBURG GABORONE
PORTSMOUTH NH (USA) CHICAGO MEXICO CITY SAO PAULO

Designed by Celia Floyd
Illustrations by Alan Fraser (Pennant Illustration) and Hardlines (map p.6)
Colour reproduction by Dot Gradations.
Printed in Hong Kong / China

01 00 99 98
10 9 8 7 6 5 4 3 2 1

ISBN 0 431 02859 1

British Library Cataloguing in Publication Data

Robinson, Claire
Chimps. – (Really wild)
1. Chimpanzees – Juvenile literature
I. Title
599.8'844

This book is also available in a hardback library edition (ISBN 0 431 02858 3)
Flick the pages of this book and see what happens!

Acknowledgements
The Publishers would like to thank the following for permission to reproduce photographs:
ARDEA London Ltd, p.5 left (Jean-Paul Ferrero), pp.11, 22 (Adrian Warren);
BBC Natural History Unit/Gerry Ellis, p.9;
Bruce Coleman Ltd, p.15 (Peter Davey), p.4 right (Jorg & Petra Wegner);
NHPA/Jeff Goodman, p.5 right;
Oxford Scientific Films, pp.4, 7, 10, 16 (Mike Birkhead), pp.13, 14, 17, 18, 19, 20, 21, 23 (Clive
Bromhall), p.12 (Jackie Le Févre/Survival), p.6 (Michael W. Richards), p.8 (Richard Smithers).
Cover photograph: Oxford Scientific Films/Clive Bromhall

Our thanks to Oxford Scientific Films for their help and co-operation in the preparation of
this book.

Contents

Some words are shown in bold, **like this**.
You can find out what they mean by
looking in the glossary.

Chimpanzee relatives

Chimpanzees, or chimps, are a type of **ape**. The animals you can see here are all apes.

chimpanzee

gibbon

gorilla

orang-utan

Apes have long, strong arms. Unlike monkeys, they don't have a tail.

What's it like to live in a family of chimpanzees?

Where chimps live

Chimpanzees live in central and west Africa. They like hot **tropical** forests and grassland.

Their hands and arms are strong for
climbing and swinging from tree to tree.
Their feet have thumbs, which help
them to grip branches.

The family

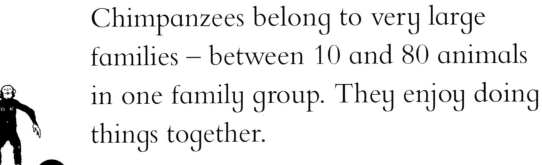

Chimpanzees belong to very large
families – between 10 and 80 animals
in one family group. They enjoy doing
things together.

These chimps are **grooming** each other gently with their fingers. Grooming helps the **apes** to make friends in the group. It is also restful.

Night and day

During the day, most chimpanzees travel on the ground. Notice how they walk on their feet and their **knuckles**.

At night they climb up into the trees to
sleep. They bend branches and leaves
over to make a comfortable nest.

Eating

This mother and her baby have gone off by themselves to look for food. Chimps like seeds, young leaves and insects.

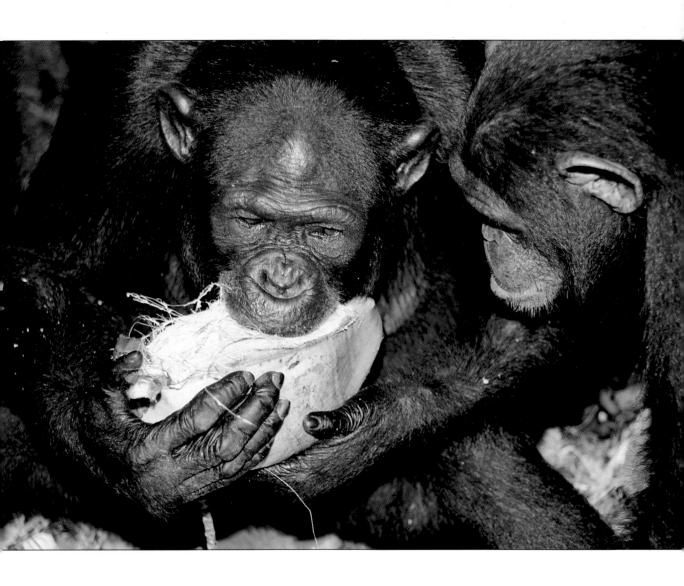

But most of all, they enjoy the taste of ripe fruit. They spend up to four hours a day searching for this delicious food.

Sticks and stones

Sometimes nuts and fruit have a hard
shell. The clever apes use stones
to break them open.

Ants and **termites** are a treat too! This female carefully lifts termites out of their nest with a thin stick. She eats them quickly before they can bite.

Babies

The mother carries her baby until it is nearly four years old. The tuft of white hair on its bottom shows that it is a baby, and reminds the family to treat it gently.

Babies spend many hours playing, just like us. Their pink ears and faces become darker as they grow older.

Growing up

This six-month-old baby is learning
fast. Perched on her mother's back,
she watches how her uncle eats fruit.

Chimpanzees must also learn how to **communicate** with each other. This young chimp is hooting to let others know where he is.

Getting angry

Another chimp has annoyed this male. He is making a lot of noise. Look how his hair is on end!

When chimpanzees show their teeth like this, they are not happy.

Why do you think the mother is angry?

Chimpanzee facts

- Chimpanzees live for about 40 to 50 years.

- Male chimps can be **aggressive**. They scream, beat the ground with their hands and throw sticks at each other.

• Chimps eat mainly fruit, and some leaves and insects. They enjoy meat, and sometimes hunt monkeys and wild pigs.

• Chimps can use tools, like sticks and stones. Very few animals can do this. Chimps can even make a sponge out of leaves and bark. They use it to soak up water for drinking.

• Chimpanzees are in danger. People cut down the forests where they live. Many young chimps are trapped and sold to collectors.

Glossary

aggressive   someone who fights and shouts is aggressive

apes   animals like chimpanzees, with hands and no tail

communicate   give others information and let them know what you think and feel

grooming   tidying and cleaning hair and skin

knuckles   the parts of your fingers that bend

termite   insects a bit like ants

tropical   in the hot and rainy parts of the world

Index